D0403289

SHOESTRING CHIC

SHOE STRING CHIC

101 ways to live
the fashionably
luxe life for less

Tips and Illustrations by
Kerrie Hess

Guilford, Connecticut
An imprint of Globe Pequot Press

To buy books in quantity for corporate use
or incentives, call **(800) 962-0973**
or e-mail **premiums@GlobePequot.com**.

skirt!® is an attitude . . . spirited, independent, outspoken, serious, playful and irreverent, sometimes controversial, always passionate.

Project editor: Kristen Mellitt
Illustrations by Kerrie Hess © Kerrie Hess

Library of Congress Cataloging-in-Publication Data is available on file.

ISBN 978-1-59921-988-2

Printed in China

10 9 8 7 6 5 4 3 2 1

"Chic is about confidence and originality—like wearing one thing that really stands out from the crowd, such as a pair of vintage sunglasses. A chic look should always be easy, effortless, and fun."

—Noah Dreier

Deputy Art Director, *Glamour*

DEDICATION

To Pippa Masson and Mary Norris for believing in this book from the very beginning. Your advice and encouragement along the way have been invaluable and inspiring.

To Mum and Dad, for showing me how to enjoy the little things in life from day one. To Meg, for being my best friend and tipping me off on custom fragrances in New York and getting me acquainted with the joys of Century 21 and brunch at Bergdorfs. And to my other best friend Tom. You are an amazing brother, who happens to make me laugh and save lives for a living. Also to Seb, for encouraging me to write this book, and for your attempted fashion illustrations. Nothing makes me laugh more.

To the international style makers that have all kindly contributed to *Shoestring Chic:* Lulu Guinness, Collette Dinnigan, Gail Elliott, Heidi Middleton, Jemma Kidd, Kelly Hoppen, Kelly Wearstler, Deborah Lloyd, Stephanie Phair, Lee Pears, Jo Upfill-Brown, Yasmin Sewell, Sarah-Jane Clarke, Alex Spring, Alicia Moodley, Peter Alexander, and Alison Chow. You all prove that a sense of chic is indeed learned or instinctive rather than bought, through your own sense of style.

And finally to the very little man in my life: Marcel. You have taught me that time with you to simply blow raspberries and run around in the park on a sunny day is truly my greatest luxury.

FOREWORD

According to fellow comedian Jerry Seinfeld, it was George Burns who muttered on his death bed that the secret to life is a combination of three things: "Falling in love, working your ass off, and paying attention."

For me, it's *paying attention* that stands out from George's wise words: The first crack of a crème brûlée's burned-sugar top. Sipping the perfect creamy cappuccino midmorning. Pulling on a pair of fluffy cashmere socks on a cold flight. Biting into a super-sweet macaroon at Ladurée in Paris, with absolutely nowhere else to be. Slipping on your favorite lounge wear for a winter's night of staying in with a big bowl of popcorn and a date with a face mask. Phone *officially* off the hook.

Little moments when you are really paying attention can feel more indulgent than dripping in diamonds.

As an international fashion illustrator with an obsession for all things beautiful, I have never believed that money *alone* can buy style.

To me, life and a sense of chic are indeed all in the details . . .

LULU GUINNESS
FASHION AND ACCESSORIES DESIGNER

"Chic is all about creating a style that is uniquely yours. . . .
Don't be a slave to fashion and never take fashion
or yourself too seriously."

INTRODUCTION

Do you suffer with the affliction of Gucci taste on a Gap budget? Do you dream about Temperley but live in Target? With the world economy forcing almost everyone to pull in her Pucci purse strings, there is even more reason to seek out life's *little* luxuries, reinvent what you already own, and simply buy better.

There is nothing at all chic about wearing the latest Prada pencil dress, while drowning in debt. But *is* there a way to live *la dolce vita* without a wardrobe full of *la Dolce and Gabbana?* Indeed there is.

Cunning stylists and designers have always known that you don't need to spend a fortune to look chic. You just need to know where to look, and when. What to splurge on, and when to go completely cheap and cheerful.

The savvy recessionista also knows that just because she may not be staying at the Ritz in Paris, that doesn't mean she can't channel her inner Ritz with a fabulous cocktail at the hotel's Hemingway Bar, or sip café au lait at Hotel Costes like she owns the place—while *actually* staying at cheap and still very chic boutique hotel Mama Shelter for just over $100 a night.

And in many cases, luxury *is* so much more about *experience* than actual possessions. Can't spring for a new Hermes Birkin at Bergdorf in New York? Then head to the luxe Kelly Wearstler–designed BG Restaurant on level seven of said department store for coffee and lemon soufflé instead. You'll get a delicious Bergdorf experience for under a twenty, no waiting list required.

In this book I'll show you where to find cheap and chic Parisian wedding dresses, the best sample sales and online designer discounts, and the world's best flea markets. I'll even show you how to shop your very own closet. Chic on a shoestring awaits you, in 101 ways . . .

NO. 1 SHOP YOUR OWN CLOSET!

Were you just about to head out the door in search of yet another item you don't even have space for in your closet? Well perhaps you should take a proper look at what you already have (and could resurrect from the dead), before you run out and inflict any more collateral damage.

Take some time to examine each item in your wardrobe closely. Put on some music and try on all of your "not-sure" items to rediscover what fabulous gems you already have that you temporarily fell out of love with.

Be brutal with the items you still don't feel 100 percent about, or haven't worn for over a year. (There is *always* a reason.) Then hang and fold all of your "to keep" pieces lovingly and neatly. Send items that need a nip and tuck to the tailor and those that didn't make the cut to charity. Now enjoy a glass of wine for your efforts.

Perfect closet karma . . .

NO. 2 THE CHEAP AND CHEERFUL RULE OF THUMB

The good news for bargain hunters is that it's not *always* wrong to buy cheap clothing. The general rule is that cheap duds in bright colors usually look, well, even cheaper than they were, whereas clothes bought for a song in neutral colors generally look more expensive than their actual price (they also tend to blend in well with higher quality items). The trick is not to wear all of your bargain basics at once. For example, that ten dollar white singlet that you picked up from Target fits in nicely with a wonderfully tailored pair of quality Palazzo pants. Or those basic black footless tights with a fabulous print dress and black flats create a simple but chic look.

NO. 3 GARMENT POLICE

Even in the heat of the shopping moment, always check the garment details before you buy. Confirm the fabric and care instructions fit your budget. (Most "dry clean only" items *can* be gently washed by hand, but they can never be put through the washing machine.) Then look for any pulls in the garment, as well as good stitching and the actual fabric content. An item advertised as "cashmere blend" can sometimes contain only 2 percent of the good stuff, and any item that needs to be repaired once you get home may not be such a bargain after all.

NO. 4 WELL HEELED

Did you just purchase a wonderful, expensive pair of leather boots? Before you toss out the old ones, take a good look at all your previous pairs of boots and leather heels. Is it the sole and heel cap of the shoes that love you and leave you first? If so, don't leave your boots to be resoled and capped until it is truly too late. Do it at the first sign of wear and tear—or even better, do it *before* anything begins to turn ugly. You will feel very smug indeed as your boots really will be made for walking—and for several seasons at that. Two coats of leather spray will further enhance your leather goods for years to come.

COLLETTE DINNIGAN

FASHION DESIGNER

"Fashion is about personal style—freedom to have a sense of self. . . .
Luxe always plays an important part in my fashion
philosophy, but simple, whimsical elegance is a must!"

NO. 5 GO VINTAGE

When in need of a fabulous new outfit for an event, if you can't go straight to fashion Mecca (Chanel or Dior) with a black Amex, then vintage might be your next best bet. Finding a vintage dress that fits perfectly and looks wonderful is usually more thrilling than splurging on an equally charming dress with the price tag of a small car in a high-end boutique.

Plus, you know that your vintage piece is practically now a one-of-a-kind that almost no one (aside from the odd, sweet little old lady that has forgotten all about it) will have but you. And aside from the occasional 1970s polyester number (read, highly flammable), most real vintage garments make their modern department store equivalents pale in comparison in terms of craftsmanship and quality.

If you have time, start looking in thrift shops near you or when you travel. Or just go straight to vintage resellers, where you will pay a little bit more, but essentially all of the hard hunting work has been done for you.

NO. 6 IN THE TRENCHES

I don't know what it is, but I always manage to feel just a little bit Audrey Hepburn-esqe when I wear a trenchcoat. Even many months after having my baby boy as I *still* sport saggy maternity jeans underneath and baby drool on my top—all is forgiven with the addition of a trench.

And aside from the chic silhouette that a trench always magically gives, it's just such a practical item to own as a staple for at *least* two seasons of the year: spring and autumn. This means it's a great cost-per-wear item, one that will never date.

Now for a confession: I personally own five trenches, not counting raincoat or wool versions (which nearly became six recently after a close encounter with a chocolate satin number in Banana Republic).

Five is already too many, and I am well aware of that. But my point is that you must own at least one, preferably in black or camel (this is the best starting point). The trick is to find one that comes as close to the Burberry classic as possible (belted at just the right height, then straight to the knee) without the painful price tag. Start with Zara if you need to be frugal, or spring for a higher-end brand if you can. Just make sure your trench has some depth and soft lining for warmth if you live in a cooler climate. Cue Parisian *Funny Face* moment . . .

NO. 7 UNIQLO

A cheap and cheerful way to refresh your wardrobe is simply to update your cotton basics, such as your formerly white T-shirts and singlets—*especially* when they have turned that cruel shade of beige gray. Head straight to Uniqlo, which is Japan's answer to Gap, also located in the United States. While you are there looking for T-shirts, you may even find a cashmere cardigan or a simple pea-coat for about the price of a movie ticket. Bargain bliss.

www.uniqlo.com

NO. 8 PARIS SLEEP

Are you sick of staying in rat-infested, tobacco-smelling, sixth-floor walk-up hotels when visiting Paris? (Or is that just me?) Well there *are* some chic options that should still leave you with a little room for indiscretions of the shopping kind on Rue de Rivoli. My first pick is Hotel du Petit Moulin in Bastille, designed by Christian Lacroix, at around $250 a night. Or for an even more frugal designer stay, try the Philippe Stark–designed Mama Shelter, located in Saint Blaise, for around $100 to $150 per night. You can even skip the metro and hire a scooter to zip around Paris *Amélie* style.

www.paris-hotel-petitmoulin.com

www.mamashelter.com

NO. 9 TAG HAG

The inconvenient truth about shopping is that so many items that look and feel fabulous in an (ever so dimly lit) changing room some-how can be just plain awful when you get them home for a retry in the cold hard light of day, sans soundtrack. Or those strappy sandals that fit perfectly in the store are clearly two sizes too small at home. And when you have lost your receipt, having to fill out a million forms in order to make an exchange just isn't fun. So before hanging up your new threads at home, make sure you try them on again while the tags are still attached and receipt and bag not yet thrown away, to confirm that your in-store style moment wasn't imaginary.

GAIL ELLIOTT

Designer/Model, Little Joe NYC by Gail Elliott

"Politeness is extremely chic, and occasionally in the fashion business, it can sadly be forgotten. There is nothing nicer than receiving a bouquet of scented white flowers and a handwritten thank-you note on beautiful stationery. For me this is the ultimate in chic."

NO. 10 THINK PARISIAN

Damn, those French lasses, with their sharp tailoring and their little espressos, just always look so chic. Their secret? My theory: Parisian apartments are smaller than the average maximum-security prison cell. (Although admittedly they usually have a better view, framed by pretty red flowerpots.) Hence most women in the city have unbelievably small wardrobes; just enough room for one Chanel jacket, one YSL trench, one fabulous pair of denims, and the perfect cocktail dress. No wiggle room for error in this closet, *ma cherie!* Or for average discount odds and ends in strange colors. The Parisian woman may end up rehashing the same look many times, but the result will always be chic. French femmes usually prefer a well-worn Dior to a new but quickly forgotten department store find every time.

We with the bigger closets can really learn something from this theory of controlled selection. Edit your wardrobe like a Parisian woman would, and you will only have your absolute best and chicest choices left—and probably a little more money to spend per item.

NO. 11 KNITWEAR INTERVENTION

Put down the polyester sweater and step away from the garment, very, very slowly. Poly-cotton will leave you freezing in winter and sweating like a pig in summer. Your new knitwear mantra is natural fibers . . . natural fibers. Pure cotton in summer, then lambswool, merino wool, or cashmere (if you can spring for it) in winter. These fabrics will love you back, feel softer and lighter (yet ironically warmer) to wear, and save you money in the long run.

NO. 12 CENTURY 21

So you are visiting New York, and you have scribbled in your diary that one of your must-visit destinations is designer bargain emporium Century 21. A few words of warning before hailing a cab to head downtown. Century 21 is no laughing matter. (In fact, I actually cried on the way out, it was such a stressful experience.) Let me explain. When you are talking about a $585 Pucci top marked down to $35, and you have spotted it at the same time as another shopper, things can—and will—get ugly.

At Century 21, you can only try on a few items in the changing room without having to rejoin the never-ending line. The staff treat shoppers like out-of-control prison inmates, and the haphazard displays of merchandise are constantly refreshed with new items by the hour. (This will haunt you back in your hotel room as you rock yourself to sleep after a visit. What if they have just put out a Dior dress in your size for $10?)

If you are not a good shopper under pressure, Century 21 may not be for you. But if you love to hunt around to find a diamond in the rough (and there is a lot of "rough"), then get in early before other shoppers have gotten their game on. May the Halston hunting begin . . .

NO. 13 SHOPPING EXORCISM

What I am about to suggest may sound distressing at first. There is no doubt about it. But if you really need to save your pennies, a controversial idea does exist: Don't go shopping at all. I know, distressing, but it is effective. After all, expecting yourself to be virtuous while actively looking through your favorite boutiques is like expecting a hungry lion to only play with a kitten—it ain't going to happen. A foolproof (and equally enjoyable) shopping diversion is to meet up with a friend for a coffee instead or take yourself to your favorite cafe and languish over something utterly delectable while poring over a magazine or a good book. These options are much less expensive than bingeing on Balmain, and usually a little time to yourself can be the biggest luxury of all.

SARAH-JANE CLARKE
"Sass" of fashion label Sass & Bide

"Staying chic while travelling is a challenge for even the most prepared. . . . I swear by my cashmere throw and possum boots for a good rest while flying, and a picture of my two boys to feel like home!"

NO. 14 THE TREND SPEND VERSUS FASHION GUILT

Certain trends exist purely to make us feel foolish once the look has passed—especially when we realize that we actually *paid money* to essentially look ridiculous. Trends that generally look good only in the fashion world rather than in the real world include super-high-waisted jeans, hot pants, microminis, acid-washed anything, and tulip and bubble skirts.

If you find yourself unable to control the need to embrace a trend you are pretty damn sure won't last even a second season, try to limit yourself to a cheap accessory like a scarf or earrings. Of course it's possible that you *may* end up loving said item, and wear it for years to come, but more than likely the final destination for those white lace leggings will be your local charity shop. (And at least if they only cost you $20, your fashion guilt will be minimal.)

NO. 15 TATI

Could you ever imagine that in Paris you might find a wedding dress (straight or puffball) for less than $100? Welcome to the world of Tati. Located in the urban quartier of Rochechouart, just a stone's throw from the Moulin Rouge, are five levels of überdiscount shopping all under one crowded and chaotic roof. Tati boasts suits for men for around $50, lingerie sets for $6, and children's wear for about $4 apiece. And then, within the dedicated Tati Mariage department, is an array of wedding dresses at equally insane prices, as well as diamond rings to the tune of about $400. The dresses on display are clearly not straight off Vera Wang's runway, but some of the simpler styles certainly don't look like they are from a discount warehouse either.

Then, at your wedding back home, when all your guests are gushing over your dress and asking where you bought it, you'll be smug knowing that the money you saved will cover your five-star honeymoon week in the Maldives. And you can also honestly say, "Oh, it's just something I picked up in Paris . . ." Your secret will be safe with me.

NO. 16 NYC CHIC ON THE CHEAP

The accommodations in style-city New York are notoriously expensive. And if overpriced blockbuster hotel chains make you want to cry (and The London or St. Regis are out of your league, so to speak), you may find some joy with the NYC Hotels group. Ameritania or Moderne in Times Square, The Bently uptown, or The Marcel downtown all boast chic lobbies without a pastel watercolor painting in sight. The rooms are simple but well equipped, and all are offered at cheap and cheerful prices.

www.nychotels.com

NO. 17 SWAP TEAM

Do you have some barely worn items in your closet that you can't seem to part with (perhaps their prices are still ringing in your ears), but you don't feel ready to give them over to charity? Your answer is an organized swap night. Your clothes will be checked in for token value on entry, letting you then rummage through other people's swapped items to find a treasure of your own of the same value. While I don't think I have ever actually come away from one of these events with something great, I had a fantastic night, sipped champagne, and enjoyed watching my own things go home to a happy swapper.

NO. 18 THE BIG TICKET

When on the hunt for a big-ticket item such as a wool coat or leather boots, ask yourself if you really need it at the start of the season. If you can make do for a month or two, stalk your item and wait for the sales. Coats and boots usually get slashed by at least 50 percent in the middle of winter, as do swimsuits and resort pieces halfway through summer. Call it delayed gratification, but if your piece is a timeless classic, you won't mind stretching out until next season to really wear it. Your favorite new piece will be just waiting in the wings, every time you open your closet.

KELLY HOPPEN

INTERIOR DECORATOR

"For me, the word *chic* stands for subtle and clean elegance in a home. Simple and clean lines, subtle neutral colors, and the use of exquisite materials are a perfect and easy way to achieve a look that is chic, timeless, and can be adapted to trends and seasons."

NO. 19 STATEMENT BLING

You have a last-minute cocktail function and no time or cash to spring for a new cocktail dress?

Whether costume or the real deal, nothing gussies up a simple dress that you already own better than some statement bling. (This works especially well with that forgotten little black dress lurking in the back of your closet.) A fabulous cocktail ring and detailed necklace, or a pretty cuff and some sparkly earrings, worn with an elegant updo and polished makeup will upgrade an otherwise simple dress.

Just don't do it all at once, or you may end up looking more *Christmas tree* than *Christian Lacroix*. Also steer clear of necklaces and earrings altogether if your dress already has some incorporated bling around the neckline.

NO. 20 BUFF AND POLISH

It has to be said that the most simple of outfits always look more elegant and expensive when combined with polished shoes, tended nails, and a well-coiffed head of hair. These elements don't necessarily cost the earth, but do require a little time and effort. A little personal polish will put a spring in your step and pull a basic outfit together, even if it's only for yourself.

NO. 21 WEB WONDERLAND

The clever team at luxury e-tailer net-a-porter.com have created shopping nirvana with their online sale incarnation, theOutnet.com. (Think Century 21, without the hassle of trawling through seas of faulty and marked goods, or having to physically fight it out with a fellow shopper over that last Temperley caftan, which *you saw first*.)

TheOutnet.com offers designer goods that can be purchased with all the trimmings and fabulous service of the net-a-porter.com brand, but with some major discounts. Site highlights are the *fabulous flash sales* and the weekly *going going gone sales,* where you can secure items as their price literally drops before your eyes. And honestly, what could be better than discount-designer buying in your pajamas, without a shopping line in sight? Another site to try is shopbop.com—enjoy!

www.theoutnet.com

www.shopbop.com

NO. 22 HAUTE HANDBAG

Do you already own a wonderful and quality handbag that you have cruelly abandoned because the strap length is out of date? (Most bags produced in the 1990s, for example, sported a long and impractical strap.) Why not bring the bag into this century by having your local shoe repairer shorten or adjust the strap? You'll fall back in love with that bag for about $10 to $20.

NO. 23 THE TIGHTS AND TURTLE

You can almost double your wardrobe simply by owning a quality pair of black footless (and opaque) tights and a slim-fit black wool turtleneck sweater. These items work particularly well with that shift or smock dress you had reserved only for summer. Also add footless tights under a shirtdress in spring, or a long cardigan (that covers your derriere) in autumn. You can also easily pare back that minishift or cocktail dress with black opaque tights and black flats or boot heels.

NO. 24 HEAD TO THE BACK

Most stores keep their shiny new collections out front and their dirty little sale racks at the *very* back of the store. Higher-end stores in particular tend to almost *hide* their sale racks, so head to the rear if you are hunting for a bargain. Just remember always to check these sale items thoroughly for makeup marks and pulls.

NO. 25 THE SCARF EFFECT

A beautiful print scarf (whether Pucci Italian silk, or just a pretty and inexpensive nylon version from a chain store) is one versatile little accessory. A scarf takes up very little space in your wardrobe, and it will brighten up an otherwise plain ensemble. Tie one round your neck, in your hair, or onto your handbag. That's maximum mileage from the one accessory, which is also the perfect featherweight item to take on vacation.

The high-end silk varieties tend to sit and feel a little better around the neck than the cheaper versions, but occasional gems can still be found at H&M and The Tie Rack.

NO. 26 WHAT YOUR MAMA GAVE YOU . . .

Does your mother (or even grandmother) have a secret stash of clothes that she wore in her heyday that have now done a full circle and are just ready to be rescued and brought back to life by you?

Often the trick to pulling off a vintage item is to pair it with something modern, such as your aunt's fabulous print caftan with your black cigarette pants. Or just simply make some minor alterations. That vintage silk cocktail dress may only need a nip here and a tuck there (or those puffy sleeves removed) to be completely transformed.

Because chances are that your Mom or Nana wore some seriously wonderful threads that may be just waiting to be out on the town again. (Just make sure that your grandmother approves of your intended adjustments to her beloved Ossie Clark poncho.)

YASMIN SEWELL

CHIEF CREATIVE CONSULTANT, LIBERTY OF LONDON

"Chic is something quite difficult to put into words. However, the
beautiful Jessica Lange in *Tootsie* probably sums it up perfectly!"

NO. 27 HAUTE HOTEL

If you can't spring for an interstate or overseas vacation, but still crave a luxe little getaway, why not try a hotel minibreak in your own city? When you cut out taxis, long drives, and flights, you have already saved a big portion of your holiday expenses, time waiting around, and questionable plane food. Websites such as lastminute.com have some of the country's best hotel rooms at bargain-basement prices, which can be around 60 percent off the regular rates. That means you can easily score a five-star hotel for next to nix. Check in early and lounge around the hotel pool with a cocktail. Or throw on the in-room robe, pour a long bath, and order something fabulous from room service. Do the kinds of things you probably never take the time to do at home. Bargain bliss at your finger tips . . .

http://us.lastminute.com

NO. 28 FLAT OUT

Most stylists would agree that sky-high heels with no ankle strap lengthen the leg more than any other shoe. This is absolutely true. But unless you have an on-call driver and a personal assistant, it's fairly hard to conduct your day in this kind of footwear. Your comfortable yet still stylish substitute is the ballet flat: überchic with pencil-leg black pants or dark denim jeans, yet still practical enough to run after a speedy toddler or get to work on time. The trick is to find a pair where you are showing a little "toe cleavage," which is more flattering to the foot than total coverage. If you can't splurge on a pair of classic beige and black Chanels, then try the London Sole stores in Santa Monica and San Francisco or order online. Australian label Sambag also makes adorable ballet flats in an array of delectable colors and will ship to the United States for about $40.

www.londonsole.com

www.sambag.com

No. 29 Flight Fabulous

Even when you're not flying at the pointy end of the plane, you can still feel a little sense of luxe on your travels by changing into a pair of cashmere socks and soft slipper shoes once onboard (as it's advisable to have *something* underfoot when trudging bleary-eyed to the bathroom in the dark). Then use a cashmere wrap to snuggle up in, or to fold as a makeshift pillow. Wonderful inventions to help block out the noise of an unruly cabin are earplugs and a little silk eye cover. Sweet dreams . . .

No. 30 Pledge to Le Pliage

Do you lust after the look of the latest designer leather bag, but realize when picking it up that it weighs a ton even *before* you have stuffed it with all your (*completely necessary*) day-to-day items? And then there is the heavy-duty designer price tag to contend with . . .

Enter Longchamp's Le Pliage. With humble beginnings in France in 1948 of basic leather crafting, the Longchamp brand has become instantly recognizable since the introduction in 1993 of the Le Pliage line. All Le Pliage bags are light as a feather (being made from durable nylon and leather), foldable, and come in a wide range of colors. The classic design is perfect for everyday use as well as travel. Look out for the frequent designer Le Pliage collaborations, which are usually only produced in a limited number. Bags in the Le Pliage line start under $100.

www.longchamp.com

NO. 31 MANI-CURE

Do you have a French manicure addiction that you can't seem to kick, even though it's costing you a small fortune? Investing about $20 in a basic manicure polish set (especially if you can find one that has a specially contoured tip on the white brush) makes it easy to *almost* re-create the salon job at home. And by doing a homemade mani, you will avoid chipping your nails with your car keys *right* as you leave the salon.

NO. 32 SIMPLE CHIC

The quickest way to upgrade your pad without a penny is simply to clear out the clutter. Take one room at a time, and you will likely find ten oddball items that you have no idea why you even own, let alone are still hanging onto. Go around your home with garbage bags, fill them up, and drop them off at your local charity store.

Now that those strange porcelain figurines are gone, the next step is to display only the items that you *love* to look at, and find concealed but still practical places to hide the ugly side of life, such as keys, bills, paperwork, cords, and remote controls. Without all of the visual clutter, your home environment will suddenly feel serene and instantly so much more chic, without your having spent a cent.

STEPHANIE PHAIR

DIRECTOR, theOutnet. com

"Mix and match pieces from current and previous seasons—you can look up to date at half the price with a little clever accessorizing."

NO. 33 THE REGIFT

What to do when Aunt Mavis gives you a well-intentioned but incredibly hideous Christmas reindeer sweater? Or when you happen to receive three copies of the same CD for your birthday? Enter the regift.

Only regift an item if it is something that you would have honestly purchased for someone else in the first place. (Sadly your best friend probably won't want the reindeer sweater either.) Then regift only when all tags and packaging are still attached. And finally, make very sure not to regift an item to the person who originally bought it for you, as clearly *that* could be a little awkward.

If you can't legitimately regift, it's best to give the present straight to charity, knowing that someone else will likely appreciate it so much more.

NO. 34 IN THE NAVY

Channel Coco Chanel's simple resort style with a few navy and white stripes. A classic boatneck cotton top, a pair of straight shorts if you have the legs for them, or a lightweight tailored blazer in bold or seersucker stripes adds some instant St. Tropez chic to a summer look.

Navy-striped knit cardigans and sweaters are also a fall and winter staple that will never date. Think Audrey Hepburn in *Roman Holiday,* or Audrey Tautou in *Coco Avant Chanel.*

Navy stripes are traditionally worn with gray, black, white, or red. Or try teaming them up with brights or prints for a more eclectic look.

NO. 35 TOPSHOP

A brand that sells twenty-five hundred dresses a day, as well as forty thousand pairs of shoes every week, must be doing something right. Although the biggest and the best Topshop store is the Oxford Circus flagship in London, you can still get hold of great Topshop wares either by legging it to the New York store in Soho or buying your spoils online (where shipping is a flat rate of $15 to any U.S. address and delivered in seven working days). Topshop collection highlights are jackets, lingerie, and shoes, as well as the embellished Kate Moss collection.

us.topshop.com

NO. 36 DO THE DIFFUSION

A diffusion fashion line such as Stella McCartney for Target, or Karl Largerfeld for H&M is a great opportunity for those who adore Stella and Karl's original designs, but really can't afford to pay a thousand dollars for a designer gray cardigan or a ruffled white shirt. A diffusion version from a chain store delivers a similarly cut piece, for about a tenth of the price of an original, with the main difference being the quality of fabric used in the chain-store line. Stick with diffusion lines from actual fashion designers (rather than celebrity lines), and you may just find some wonderful wardrobe additions for a super-small price.

NO. 37 THE POWER BALM

There are some beauty products that are beauty-editor cult favorites for good reason. The adorably tin-packaged Rosebud Lip Salve is one of them. Selling since 1895, this multipurpose balm has been used to treat dry lips, cracked skin, and minor burns for 115 years. Perfectly pretty and compact enough to always have one in your handbag, all for around $6. In Australia, Lucas Pawpaw ointment is a similarly fabulous minitube of ointment made of fermented papaya, which also packs a big punch as a lip balm and all around dry-skin saver for about $5.

www.smithsrosebudsalve.net   www.lucaspapaw.com.au

NO. 38 VINTAGE RESELLERS NYC

Can't quite afford that new Balenciaga wool coat? Well, you just might find one in a lightly preloved state at a designer resale consignment store in the major city closest to you. Check out DecadesTwo and The Way We Wore in Los Angeles, Designer Resale stores on 81st Street in New York, or Eskell in Chicago. Or seek out your local Buffalo Exchange (of which there are thirty-seven stores across the United States), where you can trade in your own unwanted pieces for store credit. Even better are rummage sales or rare vintage stores off the beaten path (yet still somewhat near you) that no one has found out about yet, as their prices will be well below the well-known vintage sellers.

www.decadestwo.com

www.thewaywewore.com

www.designerresaleconsignment.com

www.eskell.com

www.buffaloexchange.com

NO. 39 WHEN TO FLY

Tuesday, Wednesday, and Saturday are usually the cheapest days to fly. The crack of dawn, midnight, and lunch time are the least expensive times, as unsurprisingly most people prefer to fly midmorning or at the end of the business day.

If you are booking flights well in advance, the major carriers often have better prices than the low-cost airlines, which become a better value at the last minute. So whenever it's possible, book early, avoid flying around national holidays, and be flexible with your dates and times.

Deborah Lloyd

Co-President and Creative Director,
Kate Spade New York

"Chic is the confidence to follow your own path, to wear what makes you smile, and to break the rules!"

NO. 40 WHEN TO INVEST

When it comes to the classic items in your wardrobe—such as a fabulous cocktail or evening dress, tailored black pants, or your go-anywhere tailored jacket—it's usually best to invest. You will be (hopefully) wearing these items for *years* to come, and there are certain designers who just have a knack for creating garments that wear well, in styles that never date. Dresses from Oscar de la Renta, Collette Dinnigan, Dior, Chanel, and Vivienne Westwood stand the test of time.

Suiting by Stella McCartney, Helmut Lang, or Armani is always chic. Try vintage resellers if the originals are out of the question. Brands such as Karen Millen, Joseph, Jigsaw, JCrew, and Banana Republic are also wonderful at creating classic, timeless styles with quality fabrics and cuts.

NO. 41 ALL IN THE DETAILS

Nine times out of ten, if your handbag and shoes are chic, then the rest of your ensemble will look reasonably chic too. However, on the opposite scale, a great dress with plastic shoes and a pleather handbag can't usually be revived. So much of a chic look is in the accessories. Think about spending a little more on the bag you will be carrying all season long and the shoes you will be zipping around in most of the time, as well as the other accessory staples you use every day. A great watch and a chic wallet, for example, are worth splurging on.

NO. 42 IN-JEANIOUS

Jean styles will come and go, but if you can afford to invest in only one great pair, then the most universally flattering style is a dark denim boot cut or straight leg, with a midrise waist, and very little other detail. Wide- and pencil-leg styles are wonderful if you have long legs. Also look for large-size back pockets that sit quite low.

Finding the right jeans that shape your derriere and fit like a glove, but still let you sit down and actually breathe, can be harder than shopping for a flattering swimsuit (which most women would agree can be worse than attending your own funeral). Take the time to find that elusive pair of perfect jeans, as it's perhaps the wardrobe staple that you will be slipping into more than any other.

NO. 43 THE FASHIONABLE HOME

I have to admit to having a major style-crush on decorating maven Kelly Wearstler for her bold color combinations and Art Deco styling in home decor. Look to Kelly's style when you want to bring a sense of *fashion* and downright *glamour* to your home. The Wearstler sensibility is for those not afraid of strong colors, prints, and metallics. Splurging on just one designer piece per room, even if the rest of your home is decorated with simple but timeless basics, can have a major impact on your space for a fairly minor outlay.

www.kwid.com

NO. 44 THE BEST-EVER BEAUTY PRODUCT

Despite all of the wonderful tales of moisturizers that have been harvested at the bottom of the ocean, or blessed by devout monks in the Italian countryside, there is still nothing that will do more for your skin than regular sunscreen from your local drugstore. (Although admittedly, monks and deep-sea diving sound a lot more interesting.) Save a fortune on antiwrinkle lotions and potions by slathering yourself in sunscreen instead. Do it whenever you're heading outdoors, regardless of how late in life you start doing so, with a *broad-spectrum* sunscreen of the highest factor you can find. A wide-brim hat and a lightweight caftan cover-up are also great sun-exposure essentials that will do more for your skin than any $400 miracle cream.

NO. 45 A LITTLE SECRET IN BRICK LANE, LONDON . . .

When staying in London, try to be free on Sunday from 8 a.m. to 2 p.m., when the eclectic neighborhood of Brick Lane houses a fabulous market full of hidden treasures such as antiques, vintage bicycles, and clothing. (This is a more bargain-worthy market than the charming but expensive Notting Hill Markets.) Brick Lane is also home to UK-based Designer Sample Sales. Sign up in advance on their website, and you will receive an invitation to the trimonthly designer sample sales events. Just expect to fight it out for major designer labels at amazing discounts.

www.designersales.co.uk

NO. 46 EBAY

Even if the initial excitement behind eBay has now died down, the online auctioneer is still a great site to offload those pieces in your wardrobe that no longer fit or you have simply fallen out of love with. Make your sale items pop out by keeping in mind the following tips:

- Use clear, well-lit images.

- Be concise and complete in your item description. Use short sentences that are easy to read, including specific details about the item such as dimensions, shipping, and payment.

- If your item is of the label variety, include a close-up shot of the label, as well as any tags and certification stamps available.

- Search for similar items that are already listed on eBay to inform your price strategy.

- Be honest about the condition of your goods, or be prepared to face some nasty feedback once your seller has received your items!

www.ebay.com

LEE PEARS
ART DIRECTOR, *TATLER*

"Once I stopped spelling it with a *sh* (typical designer), I realized that chic can be whatever you want it to be. It's getting it right that's the key. For me, Audrey Hepburn is the epitome of chic."

NO. 47 LIP SERVICE

A simple way to add a sense of chic and polish to your look is with a well-applied slick of red lipstick. As red lips are so dramatic, they often can have more impact on your look than sparkly diamond earrings or even a pair of new-season Jimmy Choos. Work red lips at night, along with very little eye makeup other than mascara. For a first flirt with red lips, try a rouge-stained gloss and work your way up to a full-fledged crimson pout. A red hue to match almost every skin tone on the planet can be had at M·A·C for around $15.

www.maccosmetics.com

NO. 48 HOTEL HOME

If you love that calm and serene feeling of swanning back into your chic hotel room when on vacation, then why not replicate that styling at home? For a hotel look, stick to bold, neutral-toned pieces in a chic palette of white, gray, beige, and black. Clear away clutter and add some metallic touches for a hint of glamour, such as a statement pendant lamp, vase, or sculptural piece. Designer Kelly Hoppen offers ideas for the ultimate in minimal hotel chic styling, such as opting for an all white (or black-and-white) duvet cover and linens in the bedroom.

www.kellyhoppenretail.com

NO. 49 SALES TACTICS

Ever noticed that during sale times at your favorite shop there suddenly appears to be a number of items—now all 50 percent off—that you have never seen before, even though you may have stalked the store all season long? Unfortunately many stores, even at the higher end of the market, manufacture items especially *for* sale times. These items are usually of a lower quality than the store's core stock. You can often spot this kind of garment, as it will be available in large quantities and in a cheap fabric. Unless you happen to love the item in question, these duds are best avoided.

NO. 50 YOUR RIGHT TO REFUND

Most sale items are nonreturnable. However, sale or not, if the item you bring home is faulty or damaged, then you are usually entitled to a full refund, provided you were not made aware of the fault at the time of purchase.

It's always best, however, to save yourself a dispute with your local boutique by thoroughly checking over any sale items before you buy. Each has likely been kicking around the store for months, and may still be unsold for a good reason.

NO. 51 STORE CARD CACHET

Store cards should generally be avoided unless you are *already* a dedicated shopper there. In that case, a store card can be put to work accruing points and discounts on items you would have bought anyway. Just always resist the urge to make purchases *only* to accrue points.

Store cards for places where you don't regularly shop will go unused, and your wallet—if anything like mine—just doesn't need any more plastic fantastic.

NO. 52 THE LBD

No self-respecting fashionista could leave her wardrobe devoid of at least one illustrious little black dress, or LBD. Chic, classic, and appropriate for almost any occasion—not to mention flattering to every skin type and figure on the planet— the LBD has become one of the single most coveted fashion pieces of modern dressing since its first design in 1926 by Coco Chanel.

A LBD need not cost a fortune. Paired up with chic accessories and some sharp styling, it will likely look much more expensive than it was. The trick is to find one with some interesting detail in the cut, or your "oh so appropriate" LBD may just be so sensible that it never feels exciting enough to wear.

NO. 53 SIMPLE SMALLS

Quality basic cotton underwear needn't cost the earth. Replace those gray and fraying undies with a new set each year for next to nix from Dim in France, Marks & Spencer in the UK, Bond's in Australia, or Victoria's Secret in the United States, whose basics in cotton or microfiber are both comfortable and long lasting.

www.dimparis.com

www.marksandspencer.com

www.bonds.com.au

www.victoriassecret.com

NO. 54 MAYBELLINE GREAT LASH MASCARA

Introduced in 1971, Maybelline's Great Lash Mascara is the number one selling mascara in the global market. The formula is water based, so this makeup artist staple removes easily and rarely clumps, all for around $5. It's no wonder its iconic pink and green packaging passes through a drugstore scanner somewhere in the world every one-and-a-half seconds.

NO. 55 CETAPHIL FACE WASH

Fragrance, foaming agents, and color additives are the main culprits in a face cleanser that cause skin reactions and breakouts. Even high-end skin-care brands can load their products with these ingredients and then sting you at the counter for the pleasure of doing so. Cetaphil face wash was originally formulated for patients with skin so sensitive that even water caused a reaction. This non-foaming, colorless, and fragrance- and soap-free product, which the majority of dermatologists recommend, can be had for less than $10. Neutrogena's Clear Pore Cleanser/Mask is another wonderful double-duty beauty buy.

www.cetaphil.com

www.neutrogena.com

ALEX SPRING

FEATURES EDITOR, *VOGUE AUSTRALIA*

"Polished red lips are the last word in timeless chic. As there is a red out there for everyone, all it takes is a little research and thoughtful application to look perfectly pulled together."

NO. 56 PALMER'S AND THE GOOD OIL

First concocted in 1840, Palmer's chocolate-scented body care line is wonderful for treating dry skin, preventing pregnancy-related stretch marks, or providing a good soak in the bath with a few drops of the body oil version. All products in the Palmer's line are insanely well priced and available at most drugstores. It's hard to find a reason not to use them, aside from the scent causing you to run for the chocolate drawer . . .

Bio-Oil is another fantastic drugstore product to use on dry skin, stretch marks, and uneven skin tones.

www.palmers.com

www.bio-oil.com

NO. 57 HAUTE HONG KONG

A cocktail at the Philippe Starck–designed Felix Bar on the top floor of the Peninsula Hotel is one of the most decadent drinks in Hong Kong. Located on the mainland harbor, with breathtaking views below, the designer space is wonderful to enjoy a predinner drink, even if you won't be springing for four courses in the adjoining restaurant afterward.

When staying on Hong Kong Island, the *Star Ferry* is an experience in itself, transporting you for less than a dollar over to the mainland harbor where the Peninsula Hotel is situated. These iconic Hong Kong ferry boats have been running across the Victoria Harbour for over one hundred years and truly capture the heart and lights of the city.

No. 58 Les Marché aux Puces, Paris

When looking for that one-off piece of luxe antique furniture for your home, the absolute best place to find it is at Les Marché aux Puces, one of Paris's many flea markets.

Take the metro to Porte de Clignancourt on Line 4, and follow the crowds toward the large concrete overpass. Rue des Rosiers is the main street to wander to access several separate markets in the area. Art Deco lamps, baroque mirrors, and original Louis chairs can all be found along the cobblestone streets. Just be prepared to haggle, and keep in mind that shipping these bargains home will likely sting your wallet quite a bit. You might want to focus on things that you can fit in your carry-on luggage, such as a vintage clock, a candleholder, or antique prints to frame later.

Hours are Saturday from 8:30 a.m. to 6:00 p.m., Sunday from 10:00 a.m. to 6:00 p.m., and Monday from 10:30 a.m. to 6:00 p.m.

NO. 59 BLOG LOVE

Fashion and style blogs are a great way to be instantly inspired right from your laptop for no fee at all. Log onto the following sites for an e-perk-me-up.

www.thesartorialist.blogspot.com www.michigirl.com.au

www.style.com

www.facehunter.blogspot.com

www.adesignaffair.blogspot.com www.cupcakesandcashmere.com

www.mamamia.com.au

www.garancedore.fr

www.instyle.com

www.designspongeonline.com

www.girlwithasatchel.com

NO. 60 FLOWER POWER

A simple floral arrangement as a room centerpiece will always spell chic, especially a large bunch in a single hue. To make your arrangement last a little longer, pick flowers that are still in bud, snip off any leaves below water level, and make a diagonal cut at the bottom of the main stem. Adding a few small drops of bleach (to counteract mold) and a teaspoon of sugar to a vase of warm water will also help prolong the life of your flowers. In terms of faux flowers, most of these are best avoided. But something like bamboo sticks in a neutral tone (or even spray painted white) displayed in a simple but bold vase can look chic and won't need to be updated like real flowers do.

NO. 61 PICNIC LUXE

Looking for a swoonworthy dining experience, but can't quite justify a night out at Nobu? Why not hit your local farmers market, and pick up a selection of your favorite antipasti nibbles, the creamiest brie you can find, a crunchy baguette, and a bottle of champagne? Treat yourself and a girlfriend or loved one to a divine picnic feast either watching the sunset at the beach or spending a lazy summer evening in the park. Who needs The Ivy? (*Major* brownie points for creativity when it's your year to organize Valentine's Day!)

ALICIA MOODLEY
ART DIRECTOR, MARIE CLAIRE

"Contemporary fashion and interiors often look to the past and when they are interpreted with an individual twist, it can only lead to a truly chic result."

NO. 62 BRAND-SPANKING SHOE

Some think of the ironically named Happy Valley area in Hong Kong as home to one of the world's most famous race courses. I however like to think of it as "strappy shoe city." When staying in Hong Kong, hop on a tram and head straight to Leighton and Wong Nei Chung Roads for thousands of pairs of fanciful footwear. There are so many shoes on display, including sample sizes, with some great bargains to be found. Just remember not to go overboard, or your shoe loot will be impossible to lug back to your hotel.

NO. 63 WHITE OUT

Keep that wonderful white shirt whiter than white by attacking stains of coffee or sweat early. Try soaking your shirt for twenty minutes in a solution of water and a quarter cup of white vinegar before washing. A baking soda paste smeared onto pesky sweat stains is another prewash trick. Your last resort is an overnight soak in diaper cleaner. Once washed, dry your whites in direct sunlight, which will also naturally whiten them.

NO. 64 ENTERTAINING IN

Throwing a lavish dinner party, or just having the girls over for a *Sex and the City* marathon, need not cost a fortune. Your first step is to head to the market to purchase any seasonal ingredients—delicious and inexpensive. Your next step is to add a couple of fabulous highlights to your menu. A homemade pizza with a drizzle of truffle oil can transform something simple into something fabulous. Serving miniversions of popular dishes can also add a little elegance to your evening. Try smaller versions of gourmet burgers, prawn rice paper rolls, pastry tarts topped with fresh fruit . . . the list is endless. For winter evenings in, a casserole such as beef bourguignonne is a delicious French feast that calls for less-expensive cuts of beef. As is the rule with most casseroles, you just need to cook the dish several hours ahead of time to tenderize the meat.

You can also theme cocktails around an alcohol that you already have at home. In doing so, all you will need to buy are mixers and perhaps a dash of lemon or lime. Fresh flowers, some scented candles, and a little Nina Simone in the background also go a long way to add a little panache to an evening of entertaining.

NO. 65 PRICE GRABBER

When you're on the hunt for a new appliance or electronic item like a digital camera or laptop, it's always wise to do some online comparison shopping. Many sites will also calculate shipping costs when you enter your zip code. PriceGrabber.com is one of the most used, but Google and Bing also have price comparison sites. (Although it's tempting to physically have a look at the item in person first and *then* go online and find the best price, remember that if you get great service at the local store, it's better to pay the extra money and keep them in business for when you come back with questions or for repairs.)

www.pricegrabber.com

www.froogle.google.com

www.bing.com/shopping

NO. 66 HIT THE BACK STREETS

When in Rome (as well as most other European cities), look for cafes that are loaded with locals rather than sneaker- and anorak-wearing tourists. These are usually off the main squares.

The bee's knees of outdoor people watching, in my humble opinion, is Rue Montorgueil in Paris. Local fashionistas strut like ponies along this well-known cafe-laden street (which still has a distinctly more local feel than cafes situated near Le Louvre). So nab the best outdoor spot you can find, and enjoy the show!

NO. 67 THE MANE EVENT

When your whole wardrobe is in a rut, sometimes a great new haircut is all that you really need to update your look. (Cue Gwyneth Paltrow's *Sliding Doors* moment.) When you have worn your hair long and layered for years, a blunt bob is a swift change that won't take long to grow out should you leave the salon in tears. Adding in a fringe or going a few color tones in either direction of your current shade can also be more invigorating than a whole new wardrobe.

KELLY WEARSTLER
INTERIOR DECORATOR

"The epitome of chic is the ability to merge fashion and accessories from a range of designers and eras to achieve a style that is entirely your own. It's all about creating a diverse look in which all of the details come together to create a spectacular moment in time."

NO. 68 MIX IT UP

When you really believe that you have *nothing* to wear, it's time to get creative. Could you give that pastel party dress a whole new look by adding a biker jacket and ankle boots? What about trying some over-the-top gold jewelry with navy and white stripes? Or mixing fierce gladiator heels with a feminine skirt? Try pairing vintage with modern, department store with designer, neutrals with bright colors. Add a belt and scarf to a shapeless black knit dress. Borrow your partner's white shirt and wear it with black leggings and a wide belt. And don't be afraid to try prints with prints, such as stripes with florals, argyle with dots. Some of the most unexpected combinations can result in your best looks yet, and tapping into your adventurous side may just double your wardrobe possibilities.

NO. 69 COACH COMFORTS

When flying a low-cost airline or in coach class, it's up to you to plan ahead and ensure that your flight is that little bit more comfortable. Most budget carriers can get quite skimpy on the entertainment offerings, so to avoid being left with nothing to do, bring your book or magazine of choice, and a charged MP3 player. Avoid that still-frozen burger or, worse, nothing at all, by packing some first-class snacks of your own: almonds and dried fruit, a fresh baguette or sushi rolls, a little dark chocolate, and an empty water bottle to fill on the plane. Bliss.

NO. 70 BET ON BLACK

The new black will eventually always be black. Even clothing found in the mall tends to look more chic in this most neutral of shades. It's almost always appropriate (apart from perhaps head to toe at the beach or at a summer wedding). Black is also wonderful at playing the straight guy while letting your accessories or other pieces do the talking. Black travels well and will likely coordinate with almost everything else you own. It's an elegant and commanding hue that will simply always be chic, which means that your all-black items will likely stay current much longer than a print dress or a bright summer top.

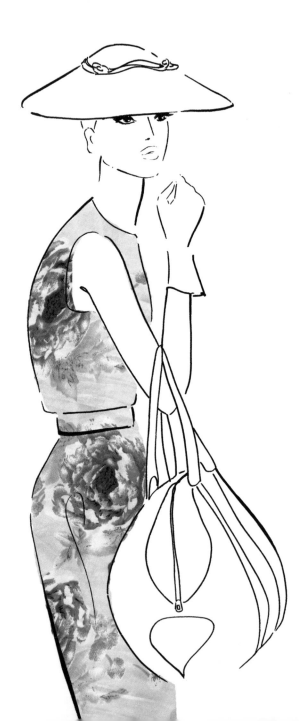

NO. 71 SUPER DE-PARLUX

Does you hair only ever look sleek and glossy when it's blown out at the salon? Do you find that you have to have your hair trimmed very often due to dry split ends? The reason for all of this bad hair karma may simply be your own hair dryer. Over time, a nasty hair dryer will do damage to your hair. A higher-quality model such as the super-lightweight, Italian-made Parlux 3500 can dry your hair in half the time of a regular hair dryer and give you a much glossier finish thanks to a ceramic and ionic system that eliminates frizz and retains hair moisture.

A salon-quality hair dryer is a great investment as it will mean fewer split ends and almost no need for hair treatments. You'll have a sleek blowout you can do at home that will look like you just stepped out of the salon after every wash.

NO. 72 SHOP FOR YOUR SHAPE

Time to forget what you wish you could change about yourself and start working with what you've got. Completely avoid splurging on trends and styles that don't suit you just because you want to play too. Great legs? A short shift dress with sleeves is your friend. Killer shoulders? Get to know the maxi dress. Décolleté to die for? Play it up with a Diane von Furstenberg wrap dress. Focus more on showing off your trump cards than on hiding your flaws.

NO. 73 BAG LADY

The best kind of investment bag is one that has a look you love, doesn't weigh a ton when empty, is well made, and has a neutral tone (although bright colors are great fun when you are completely set for black, beige, and white). Try to avoid the trendiest bags, such as the Louis Vuitton Murakami bag circa 2002, as they will date quickly. Very cheap bags generally don't last and take up too much room in the closet to justify even a modest cost. Bags that close completely, either with a zip or fold-over flap, are also a good buy, as they are much safer to hold your wallet and valuables when you travel.

Jo Upfill-brown

Art Director, *InStyle Australia*

"Chic design transcends trends . . . it is timeless. It is the classic
curve of a chair, the bold angle of a building, or the
sensual line of a shapely stiletto."

NO. 74 CHANNELING AUDREY

Capri pants, ballet flats, and a tailored boatneck knit top were the Audrey Hepburn signature look. And for "putting on the Ritz," no one can forget the long and short Givenchy LBDs in *Breakfast at Tiffany's* or the Italian-inspired ensembles of *Roman Holiday*.

But above all else, Audrey Hepburn's style was about inner elegance, as much as her passion for couture. Neutral, classic, and tailored, Audrey is the ultimate style icon. Here are some of her classic looks:

- A printed silk head scarf
- Short side-cropped haircut
- Ballet flats
- Three-quarter cropped black capri pants
- Wide-brim sun hat
- Little black (usually Givenchy) dress

You can also have yourself an Audrey moment by hitting the third floor of Tiffany & Co. on Fifth Avenue, where the less expensive but still droolworthy sterling silver items and accessories are housed.

NO. 75 I WANT CANDY

What started out as an online New York guide to local sample sales now boasts twenty-eight editions across the United States and London, as well as *Daily Candy Kids* and even *Daily Candy Weddings*. Log onto the main site for fashion, beauty, decorating, and travel deals, as well as fashion blogs, articles, and events. Or just cut to the chase and register for the Swirl Sample Sales site, which will drop you a line about local sales of up to 80 percent off in your area. Also check to see if your local city is one of the thirteen with their own dedicated Daily Candy sites. Even if you're far away, it's fun to read.

www.dailycandy.com

NO. 76 TATE-TASTIC

If art is your passion, then London is the place for you, as one of the few major cities in which most of the wonderful galleries and museums are free. The warehouse-styled Tate Modern gallery and traditional National Gallery are both beautiful spaces to inspire. Also check out the Victoria and Albert Museum for the largest number of decorative design and art pieces in the world, as well as regular fashion photography exhibitions. Then use the money you saved to splurge in the gift shops or on a long lazy lunch.

www.tate.org.uk

www.nationalgallery.org.uk

www.vam.ac.uk

NO. 77 WHAT HAPPENS IN VEGAS . . .

Designer shopping in Vegas is a world away from shopping in the überbourgeois flagship stores of New York and Los Angeles. In Vegas it's all happy shop assistants, no entry by appointments, and *major savings*.

When planning to scour for designer duds on discount here, you have two options: the Primm Valley outlets (accessible by shuttle from the MGM hotel), or the outdoor outlet mall on Grand Central Parkway. The latter has more of an upscale selection than the Primm outlets, but as it's outdoors, you will need to be ready to brave the Vegas heat in summer or be whiplashed by cold in winter. Which, for half price Bally, is probably worth it.

NO. 78 IGNORE THE SIZE

With sizing standards varying from store to store, and then also *within* most stores, it's wise to take the size you buy with a grain of salt. I have personally bought tops up to three whole sizes larger than my usual size because I prefer a certain fabric to *drape* rather than *cling*. I've also found perfectly fitting items *smaller* than my usual size when shopping in a store that has an older age target clientele. Sale racks are often also full of particular lines that were produced with incorrect sizing—good to keep in mind when you find the perfect pair of stovepipe pants, on sale, that are nowhere near your normal size; they just may fit perfectly.

NO. 79 SHRINKAGE

Generally speaking, natural fibers like cotton or wool that are put through the wash tend to shrink by about 5 percent, while 100 percent manmade fibers such as microfiber don't. So remember that the cotton T-shirt that just makes it to your belly in the fitting room will probably gift you a muffin top after just one wash. To prevent having to buy again, always purchase your cottons and wools with a *little* room for error.

JEMMA KIDD

MAKEUP ARTIST

"Things that are chic are often expensive, but to be chic is a combination of sophistication, elegance, and fashion that can never be achieved with money alone."

NO. 80 CHANNELING GRACE KELLY

Her ice-blonde tresses, coiffed into Hollywood waves or pulled back in a chic chignon, were the Kelly signature. A single strand of pearls, alongside an off-the-shoulder dress with a full tulle skirt, completed the glamourous picture.

Hitchcock's favorite muse is in full fashion flight in his films *To Catch a Thief, Rear Window,* and *Dial M for Murder.* And you know you have style when your name represents one of the world's most iconic of bags, from French fashion house Hermès. These are some Grace Kelly classics:

- Cinched belt with a full tulle or straight skirt
- Diamonds, fit for a princess
- Single strand of pearls
- Soft leather gloves

If you want to go for Grace Kelly's pearl look, here's a hint: Faux pearls are fairly easy to come by. Just look for ones where each pearl is slightly different, which will better mirror the real thing.

NO. 81 BABY CHIC

If you're dead set that your baby is to be dressed in designer threads, make sure you know it's for *you,* not for *them,* as babies generally don't know the difference between Gap and Gucci. Chain-store labels make wonderful baby clothes at affordable prices. Just be sure to focus on keeping your tot really comfortable in natural breathable fabrics like 100 percent cotton, rather than polyester. Pants with an adjustable waistband will last a season or two longer than regular pants, and jackets can always be bought a little larger than needed to really go the distance. Smock-style dresses or skirts for girls can be worn with tights or leggings as they grow taller. And any clothing of gender-neutral colors might be worth keeping for your possible next child. Target, H&M, Zara, and Gap all make afford-able, yet stylish baby clothes that will keep your little one snug as bug in a rug—as do Marks & Spencer in the UK and Bonds and Pure Baby in Australia.

NO. 82 BROOKLYN CALLING

The word is out: Brooklyn is the new shopping mecca alternative to Manhattan. Ditch the Park Avenue princess vibe, and find your inner fashionista cool in Williamsburg and Park Slope. Vintage shopping fans flock to Vintage Warehouse in "the burg" for designer duds the second time around. Hooti Couture in Park Slope is renowned for its antique accessories selection. Beacon's Closet, which you can find in both Park Slope and Williamsburg, is where you can also trade in your own unwanted goods for cash or store credit.

www.beaconscloset.com

www.hooticouture.com

NO. 83 SHOP SOLO

There are friends who will tell you that everything looks good on you just to be polite, and there are friends who just love a retail rush that comes from any direction and will encourage you to buy whatever you pull off the rack. You can love these friends, but you don't have to shop with them. When you shop solo you can selfishly try on every style in sight of the item you are looking for, and take your time when deciding yay or nay in the changing room. Then you can even beeline back for that silk scarf that you put on ice at the start of your shopping trail. Shop with friends when you are there for socializing, coffee, and a catch up; shop alone when you are on the hunt for something really particular.

NO. 84 STRAPPED FOR CASH

So you're standing in line at JCrew, handling a delicate mint green cashmere cardigan as about a million "should I, or shouldn't I" thoughts zip through your mind. The first real question you should probably be asking is "Can I pay for this with cash or debit? Or do I *have* to buy it on credit?" If you have been a holy savings saint all month and know that you can easily pay with cash—and love the item in hand—then go for it. If your already burning credit card is your only option, then it might be hard to really *enjoy* that cardigan if it causes you heartburn in order to pay it off.

NO. 85 TO MARKET, TO MARKET

Almost every major Asian city houses a fabulous night market. Examples are the ladies markets in Mongkok in Hong Kong, the night markets in Kuala Lumpur, and the Chatichak markets in Bangkok. Look for authentic locally made products and sample local cuisine from the busiest food stands while you're there. And always remember to barter. This is absolutely expected in almost all Asian markets aside from those in Japan, where bartering is not a local custom.

PETER ALEXANDER

SLEEPWEAR DESIGNER

"Any time something has a hint of Chanel to it, everyone screams that 'it is so chic'—but a real sense of chic is always *how* you wear something rather than what you wear."

NO. 86 GET BELTED

Adding two new belts to your wardrobe—or even better, locating and using ones that you already have—one wide and one slim, can double the look of your current tops and dresses. The trick is to wear them with your *larger* tops, dresses, and shirts. Extra volume and material gathering from the belt will define a waist while cleverly concealing any tummy overhang. A belt worn over a top, but under a fitted open jacket, is also a flattering chic look.

Stick to a skinny belt if you are short waisted; if you have a long torso, you can handle a thicker band. If you are a little belt shy, wear one the same color as your top or dress—such as black on black, or beige on white—as a subtle way to get started.

NO. 87 THINK MULTISEASON

The items you will get the most wear out of are the ones you can slip into almost year-round. A great white T-shirt is not only a staple in summer, but also perfect under a cardigan or sweater in the cooler months. Cotton, lightweight wool, and silk are all trans-seasonal fabrics. Linen trousers can be worn in almost every climate other than winter. A cropped jacket is chic in summer as well as when worn over a lightweight black turtleneck in cold weather. And a light cotton coat is perfect for both fall and spring, especially fun in a bright color or print, a la Kate Spade.

NO. 88 BRIDESMAID REVISITED

That puffy peach taffeta bridesmaid dress that your best friend made you wear in public ten years ago can likely be turned into a chic and, dare I say, *modern* cocktail number with only a few adjustments. If the sleeves of the dress are out of date, simply have them tailored *off*. When the length is an unflattering mid-ankle height, why not shorten it to just below the knee? Or if the color is rancid, a little packet of dye from your local drugstore could be the answer, depending on the dress fabric. For an even more incredible revamp, take a look at your prom dress; it just may also be screaming for an extreme makeover—if you're game, and it still fits!

NO. 89 DOUBLE-DUTY BEAUTY

There are so many beauty items willing to work a little overtime if required. A rose pink lipstick can also double as a dewy cheek gloss when blended in with the fingers (a healthy glow that's much quicker and easier to achieve than having to hit the gym!). A quality liquid concealer also works as an under-eye brightener, even if your beautiful baby or snoring partner actually kept you awake all night. Also try using your bronzer powder as an eye shadow in the crease of your eyelid, as a blush, and mixed with a clear gloss for a nude lip shade of an "almost no makeup" makeup look, perfect for summer.

NO. 90 KNIT PICKING

If you want your pricy knitwear to last more than a few seasons, then always fold or roll your knit garments rather than hang them, which will only distort their shape. It's also a good idea to air your wool pieces in direct sunlight before storing them through the summer, as well as when you pull them back out for fall. This will kill off any pesky odors or insect larva that may have set up camp in your favorite cardi (a disgusting thought, I know). To rid your woolies of those unwanted fabric balls, try either lightly scraping the garment with a leg razor, or, if it's your absolute best cashmere knit, five minutes gently pulling them out by hand will bring the item back to life. Remember: Always hand wash your wool items in either wool wash or baby shampoo and lukewarm water, rather than run them through the washing machine.

NO. 91 LONDON LUXE

The leafy London suburb of Kensington is home to base2stay hotel, where chic and modern apartment-style rooms are available for around $140 per night and located just a stone's throw from chic Kensington High Street. Not a piano-playing lobby or corporate pastel painting in sight. Brilliant!

base2stay.com

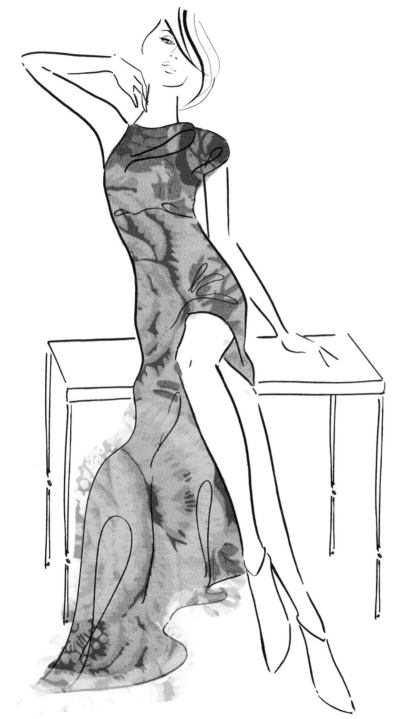

ALISON CHOW
COFOUNDER, COCO RIBBON BOUTIQUE, LONDON

"Being chic precedes fashion; it's 20 percent about what you wear and 30 percent how you put it together. The other 50 percent—that's your attitude when wearing it."

No. 92 Chic Sugar Rush

You're either a cupcake person or you're not. And should you fall into the former category, drool-worthy cupcake bakeries are popping up all across the United States, where you can usually indulge in a little cake heaven for around $2. When in New York, savor some seriously sweet and luxe cupcakes at Magnolia Bakery. There is hardly any seating in the unassuming shop, and you will likely have to face a line, but I can't think of a better way to start a shopping stroll in Greenwich Village than a turbo sugar hit from Magnolia. Fortified, you can head off to peruse the bounty of boutiques in the area including Marc Jacobs and Lulu Guinness, then on to the delights of SoHo. Also try Georgetown Cupcake in Washington, D.C., Sprinkles and Crumbs Bake Shop and a West Coast Magnolia Bakery in Los Angeles, Philly Cupcake in Philadelphia, and Society Bakery in Dallas. Primrose Bakery in London is also worth stopping in for a sweet treat and some celebrity spotting when on vacation.

www.magnoliabakery.com

www.sprinkles.com

www.crumbs.com

www.primrosebakery.org.uk

NO. 93 LUXE LUNCH

Many of the world's swankiest restaurants charge half price via a set menu at lunchtime, which is great news if you fancy yourself nibbling on sushi couture at Nobu, The Ivy, or the likes. Look for the prix fixe lunch menu at your restaurant of choice and sit back to three courses of super-posh nosh.

Brunch or an afternoon high tea is also the affordable way to sample some of the world's best eating establishments, rather than in the evening for dinner.

NO. 94 HARAJUKU HIJINKS

Tokyo's Harajuku is filled with goths wearing black nail polish and fairytale princesses in tiered tutus and sky-high platforms. And then there are *the girls,* who can be found wearing French maid outfits or dolled up like Manga cartoon characters. Aside from the visual spectacle you see by simply walking around the streets and alleyways, Harajuku is also home to an array of boutiques and markets, as well as the famous 100 Yen Store. Over five levels, this huge store houses thousands of Japanese sweets, gifts, clothing, and scented oils all for only 100 yen, which is less than $1. It's the perfect spot to pick up mini-gifts for friends back home, and some very cool and unusual keepsakes for yourself.

NO. 95 MACAROON MOMENT

When in Paris you don't necessarily have to spend a ton on Rue Cambon at Chanel, just to feel chic (although admittedly, that would be a great way to kill a morning). Some of the city's little experiences can be incredibly chic, for the price of a sugar-filled macaroon at one of the city's delectable patisseries. Start with a Coco Chanel moment at what was her favorite cafe, Café Angelena. The Chocolat Chaud Africanne is the best hot chocolate in town, which is even more delicious when poured from a haughty waiter in a tuxedo, with just the right "fluff" of whipped cream on top. Then for the most luxe patisserie on the planet, your next stop is La Durée. Linger over coffee and macaroons in this decadent tea room on the Champs-Elysées. You can also pick up lovely yet inexpensive chocolates for friends back home, all wrapped in the most divine pistachio and gold La Durée packaging.

www.laduree.fr

NO. 96 PERFUME COUTURE

So you may not be able to splurge on a little Dior couture, but what about creating your very own couture scent? Henri Bendel, Bergdorf Goodman, Barney's, and many other major stores all offer the swanky service of creating a custom fragrance. Also try Body Chemistri and Aroma Workshop in Chicago and Studio at Fred Segal in Los Angeles for a custom perfume. You can take your sweet time choosing from thousands of scent combinations, and once you have hit the jackpot, your one-of-a-kind, couture scent will be recorded in the store database for any future replacements—all for just over the cost of the latest generic celebrity perfume. Check if your local major department store or beauty boutique also offers the service.

www.henribendel.com

www.bergdorfgoodman.com

www.barneys.com

www.bodychemistri.com

www.fredsegal.com

www.aromaworkshop.com

NO. 97 LINEN LUXE

Is your linen cupboard a war zone of mismatched poly-cotton print disasters? For a hotel-quality sleep at home every night of the week, clear out those faded and downright scratchy polyester sheets, either to give to charity or to throw in the trash, and invest in at least one set of 400-plus thread count sheets, in 100 percent cotton sateen or percale. A plain neutral shade of white, ivory, gray, or chocolate should coordinate with most duvet covers. Great linen is an investment that you will spend half of your life enjoying, and it's absolutely worth splurging on.

NO. 98 INSTANT ART

When you don't have the budget to fight for an original Miro at Sotheby's, nor the artistic inclination to create your own master-piece, then perhaps that bare living room wall of yours is screaming for a black-and-white photograph. This is the easiest, cheapest way to add some visual interest to a plain wall, and black-and-white tones will match perfectly with whatever your home's decor and color scheme may be. A great print from a magazine or a personal photograph blown up and framed or printed on canvas can have major impact for a teeny tiny price. A sure hit are three black-and-white images in the same frames, hung together at an equal distance.

NO. 99 CHOCOLATE COUTURE

When you're dreaming about a little indulgence, a sampling of chocolate couture can go a long way. Authentic handmade chocolates can look as exquisite as Tiffany diamonds, and they taste a world apart from a supermarket family block. Make a date to acquaint yourself with little squares of delectable cacao heaven, screenprinted with lovely individual images at one of the country's best chocolate shops: Marie Belle in New York, Candina's Chocola-tier in Wisconsin, Recchiuti in San Francisco, or B.T. McElrath Chocola-tier in Minnesota. A chic setting for a girl's catch up (or for no reason at all, just on your own) and far less expensive than splurging at a fine-dining restaurant. A personal selection of handmade choco-lates also makes a lovely and personal gift that won't cost a fortune, with most chocolate boutiques also providing gift packaging beauti-ful enough to keep.

www.mariebelle.com

www.candinas.com

www.recchiuti.com

www.btmcelrath.com

HEIDI MIDDLETON

"BIDE" OF FASHION LABEL SASS & BIDE

"Chic travel is feeling at home in new and unfamiliar surrounds. I never leave without my goose down pillow as it fits into my carry-on and allows me to sleep beautifully on flights. Also, photos of my beautiful girls, and my rainbow bracelet, remind me of all that is extraordinary in life."

NO. 100 CHANNELING JACKIE O

Jackie O's ensemble of oversize black sunglasses with a shift dress or Chanel suit will always remain a classic combination. Add a perfectly coiffed bob with sleek square-toed low heels for the ultimate "lady of the Oval Office" look. Or just add one of the following Jackie O elements to your ensemble:

- Boatneck shift dress
- Creed Millesime perfume
- Chanel-style tweed suit
- Double-breasted box-style jacket
- Pillbox hat
- Oversize black sunglasses

A simple shift dress in either a neutral or bright shade with a kitten heel is an easy way to create the Jackie O look, as achieved by Michelle Obama via chain stores such as Gap and JCrew.

NO. 101 TIME

I've decided to save the absolute best tip for last, as no doubt the main thing you likely don't have enough of is *time*: time to indulge in your passions, time to chatter about absolutely nothing with your girlfriends, time to daydream, time to remember that you are also a woman, as well as a mother, daughter, and best friend. In this tech-mad world where most of us can always be reached by phone or e-mail, the last word in luxe is the time to actually *be unreachable*. And of course the notion of time doesn't *really* cost a thing, but it can be harder for the modern woman to get hold of than a custom-made alligator-skin Birkin in her favorite color.

We all have different priorities on our time. Reprioritizing might entail taking a step down at work, changing careers, or spending money on a cleaning person rather than a new wardrobe, just to grab hold of a little bit of the good stuff: time. Time to read the papers in bed on a Sunday morning. Time to eat ice cream in the park with your kids. Time to go on a romantic rendezvous with your partner and remember why you fell in love in the first place. Time to catch up with your girlfriends, sip cocktails, and dissect entirely frivolous but wonderful matters. Time to spend simply *on your own,* latte in hand, with absolutely nowhere to be.

After all, for all the designer goods in the world, whether on sale or at full price, the real luxury is being able to carve out a moment or two in life to *actually enjoy it.* I wish you luck.

CONCLUSION

If there is one thing that I have learned from almost every designer, stylist, and makeup artist who has kindly contributed to this book, it's that a sense of style and chic has very little to do with the joy or misery of your bank balance.

So much of looking chic comes down to *how* you wear an outfit, rather than simply *what* you wear. Feeling fabulous is the key to any look, whether your style is boho, prom princess, or gothic-punk. Confidence is *always* key.

And so too with your closet; rather than falling into the fashion rut of wearing 20 percent of your wardrobe 80 percent of the time, sometimes the most liberating thing of all is to actually *wear* those forgotten pieces in your closet that still give you butterflies. That over-the-top DVF print dress that you never have the nerve to throw on instead of your fail-safe jeans. Those gold peep-toe heels that are gathering dust, rather than your basic black sandals. Or that bright fuchsia scarf instead of your basic, everyday gray. Sometimes the best thing in the world is to *not* be neutral.

Another great mantra is to mix it up. Add some fierce platforms to that floral nana dress you were about to give away, or add a feminine belt to a man-style shirt. Try combinations in your current wardrobe that you have never dared before. Mix high street with vintage, designer with discount. Invest in your wardrobe staples, and use your intuition with the rest.

Keep it simple, know the rules, and then break them all with wild abandon!

ABOUT THE AUTHOR / ILLUSTRATOR

Australian-born Kerrie Hess has written for the *Independent* in London, and published two titles for tweens—*Girl Secrets* and *Girls Only*—as well as *The Field Guide to the Human Species*.

She has also illustrated for Chanel and Alexander McQueen, as well as for the department store Neiman Marcus.

Kerrie's work has appeared in *Vogue Australia, Tatler, InStyle,* and *Elle*. Her illustrations have also been featured on T-shirt lines in Japan, on cosmetic packaging for Bare Escentuals, in Net-a-Porter's *Notes* and on countless book covers around the globe.

She is the cofounder of lifestyle brand Femme Fatale, and has been shortlisted for a Cannes Festival Design Award in 2010.

Kerrie now lives in Melbourne, Australia, with her husband, Seb, and her son, Marcel.

Visit her website at www.kerriehess.com and her blog at www.kerrie hess.blogspot.com.